1. Introduction

The Federal Reserve's responses to the 2007-2009 financial crisis, the recession, and their aftermath included important changes in the conduct of monetary policy. The Federal Reserve rapidly reduced its target for the federal funds rate (FFR) to its effective lower bound, introduced facilities to provide ample liquidity and to maintain the flow of credit in the economy, and purchased large amounts of longer-term securities. One consequence of these changes is that the Federal Reserve will likely need to employ new tools when it begins to raise the FFR and other short-term interest rates to more normal levels.

One new monetary policy tool, the payment of interest on banks' reserves held at the Federal Reserve, has been in place since 2008. The Federal Open Market Committee (FOMC or "Committee") has indicated that interest on reserves will play a key role during the process of normalizing monetary policy (FOMC 2014c). Nonetheless, evidence in recent years indicates that the payment of interest on reserves may not provide the degree of control over the FFR and other short-term interest rates that the Committee desires, and supplementary tools might be needed to provide that level of control.

This need has motivated the FOMC to pursue the development of other monetary policy tools that might be helpful during the policy normalization process. In July 2013, Federal Reserve staff presented a proposal to the FOMC for offering reverse repurchase agreements (RRPs) to a broad set of counterparties, including nonbank institutions that are significant lenders in money markets (FOMC 2013a).[1] In concept, this innovative approach of offering RRPs at a fixed interest rate, particularly in "full allotment"—that is, satisfying any level of market demand at that rate—would help to establish a firm floor on interest rates. The FOMC directed the Desk to test variations of overnight (ON) RRP operations to learn how they could work in practice. Results of a testing exercise in place since September 2013 indicate that a facility that offers ON RRPs, even without providing full allotment, can help control short-term interest rates. Hence, a facility that offers ON RRPs with capped allotment could play an important role during policy normalization, and the FOMC has indicated that it intends to use an ON RRP facility as a "supplementary tool" as needed to help control the FFR (FOMC 2014c).

In addition to improving the FOMC's control over short-term interest rates, an RRP facility may have important secondary effects, with both positive and negative implications. In particular, an ON RRP facility could have repercussions for financial stability. These might include beneficial effects arising from the increased availability of safe, short-term assets to investors with cash management needs. However, there may be adverse effects stemming from the possibility that such a facility—particularly if it offers full allotment—could allow a very large, unexpected increase in ON RRP take-up that might enable disruptive flight-to-quality flows during periods of financial stress. In addition, very large usage of an ON RRP facility, particularly if it were permanently in place, would expand the Federal Reserve's footprint in short-term funding markets and could alter the structure and functioning of those markets in ways that may be difficult to anticipate. Indeed, FOMC policymakers have expressed concerns about a sustained

---

[1] RRPs have long been used in monetary policy implementation. Since 2009, the FOMC has undertaken preparations for the possibility of using RRPs on a larger scale.

expansion of the Federal Reserve's role in financial intermediation and the risk that ON RRPs might magnify strains in short-term funding markets during periods of financial stress (FOMC 2014a,b).

A broad understanding of an ON RRP facility's promise as a monetary policy tool, as well as its possible secondary effects—including both salutary and undesirable consequences—is therefore important as the FOMC develops plans for the normalization process and determines both the role and the specific features of an ON RRP facility. Those provisions might include features that would mitigate undesirable effects. For example, the FOMC has already indicated in its Policy Normalization Principles and Plans that the facility will be phased out when it is no longer needed to help control the FFR, and its temporary nature should mitigate some concerns about impacts on short-term funding markets (FOMC 2014c). In addition, caps on ON RRP usage could be imposed to limit the Federal Reserve's footprint in short-term funding markets or to contain potentially destabilizing inflows into the facility during periods of financial stress.

At the same time, there may be tradeoffs associated with ON RRP facility design features. For example, caps on ON RRP take-up that are too tight would reduce the degree of control a facility provides over short-term interest rates. Hence, the design of the facility will require a balancing of the tradeoffs involved in achieving the necessary degree of interest-rate control while addressing concerns about secondary effects. Notably, FOMC policymakers have generally agreed that it will be very important for the commencement of policy normalization to proceed successfully, and they have indicated that they will be prepared to take the steps necessary to ensure that the federal funds rate will trade within the target range established by the Committee (FOMC 2015).

This paper explains the potential usefulness of an ON RRP facility for implementing monetary policy during the normalization process, describes some possible secondary effects associated with ON RRPs, outlines some potential design features that could address effects that may be undesirable, and discusses tradeoffs involved in addressing those effects. The paper is organized as follows. Section 2 reviews recent changes in monetary policy that have led to the development and testing of an ON RRP facility as a monetary policy tool. We also describe the FOMC's announced intentions for such a facility and summarize the results of an ON RRP testing exercise that has been in place since September 2013. Section 3 examines some potentially important secondary effects of an ON RRP facility, including both positive and negative impacts on financial stability. In section 4, we analyze ways in which an ON RRP facility might be designed to mitigate secondary effects that could be undesirable. Section 5 discusses tradeoffs that policymakers may face in designing an ON RRP facility, as they seek to balance the objectives of setting an effective floor on money market rates and limiting any adverse effects. Section 6 offers some conclusions.

2. The ON RRP facility and its potential usefulness as a monetary policy tool

This section briefly describes the policy context for the development and testing of an ON RRP facility as a monetary policy tool and explains the rationale behind that facility. We also summarize the FOMC's announced intentions regarding the use of an ON RRP facility and review some results of an ON RRP testing exercise that has been in place since September 2013.

These tests indicate that ON RRPs may be helpful in controlling short-term interest rates when the FOMC decides to begin raising the target range for the FFR.

2.1. The operating framework for monetary policy before the financial crisis

Before the 2007-2009 financial crisis, the FOMC conducted monetary policy by setting a target for the overnight FFR—the interest rate at which depository institutions lend reserves for one day to other depository institutions—in order to influence the pricing of credit.[2] Movements in the FFR influenced other short-term interest rates, which, in turn, affected borrowing costs for households and businesses and financial conditions more broadly.

During this time, the Open Market Trading Desk ("the Desk") at the Federal Reserve Bank of New York implemented the FOMC's interest rate policy primarily by controlling the supply of reserves in the banking system. The Federal Reserve established a baseline demand for reserves by setting reserve requirements, which are minimum amounts of reserves that depository institutions must hold against their deposit liabilities.[3] In addition, banks often held excess reserves—that is, reserves in excess of requirements—as deposit balances at the Federal Reserve.

To carry out the FOMC's policies, the Desk conducted open market operations (OMOs) with designated primary dealers to adjust the supply of reserves so that, for a given level of demand, the market-clearing FFR would be consistent with the FOMC's target.[4,5] The Desk made outright purchases of Treasury securities in the secondary market and conducted temporary, "fine-tuning" operations, in the form of repurchase agreements ("repos") and RRPs in markets for U.S. government securities.[6] Desk purchases of securities from a primary dealer, whether on an outright basis or in the form of repos in a temporary operation, increased reserves because the Desk paid for the securities by crediting reserves to the primary dealer's account at the bank that

---

[2] Reserves are deposits held by banks and other depository institutions in their accounts at the Federal Reserve, as well as currency held by those institutions.

[3] All depository institutions—commercial banks, savings banks, thrift institutions, and credit unions—are required to maintain reserves against transaction deposits, which include demand deposits, negotiable order of withdrawal accounts, and other highly liquid funds. Currently, reserve requirements range from 0 to 10 percent of transaction account balances, with the 10 percent requirement applying to all balances in excess of $103.6 million.

[4] The Federal Reserve had adopted a so-called "corridor" operating framework, in which relatively small changes in the supply of reserves can have significant effects on equilibrium short-term interest rates. See, for example, Ennis and Keister (2008); Keister, Martin, and McAndrews (2008); and Kahn (2010).

[5] Primary dealers are the Desk's trading counterparties in its implementation of monetary policy. For a current list of primary dealers, see: www.newyorkfed.org/markets/pridealers_current.html.

[6] That is, the operations are carried out in markets for securities that are eligible for OMOs. These include Treasury securities, the debt of federal agencies and government sponsored enterprises (GSEs), and mortgage-backed securities backed by federal agencies and the GSEs.

cleared the transaction.[7,8] In the five years prior to the crisis, aggregate reserve supply averaged about $11 billion, of which only about $1.7 billion was excess reserves.

2.2. Federal Reserve responses to the financial crisis and recession substantially increased the supply of reserves

The Federal Reserve's responses to the financial crisis included important changes in the conduct of monetary policy as well as lender-of-last-resort actions. First, the FOMC rapidly eased the stance of monetary policy by aggressively cutting the FFR target from 5¼ percent in mid-2007 to a target *range* of zero to ¼ percent by December 2008. Second, the Federal Reserve introduced a number of facilities to provide liquidity to banks and nonbanks to maintain the flow of credit to borrowers in key markets, and to foster improved conditions in broader financial markets. Finally, with the FFR's proximity to its effective lower bound leaving little scope for further reductions, the Federal Reserve purchased longer-term securities for its securities portfolio to put downward pressure on longer-term interest rates, support the functioning of mortgage markets, and make financial conditions more accommodative.

One consequence of the Federal Reserve's actions since the financial crisis has been a sharp increase in aggregate reserve balances. In 2014, total reserves averaged $2.6 trillion, virtually all of which were excess reserves. Given the FOMC's indication that asset sales will not play a key role during the policy normalization process, reserve balances are likely to remain very large for an extended period of time.[9] With the supply of reserves far outstripping depository institutions' required reserves as well as any demand for excess reserves, modest adjustments in the supply of reserves are no longer effective in controlling the FFR. Indeed, the Desk has not conducted OMOs to manage the supply of reserves since December 2008. Thus, new tools are required to provide effective control of the FFR.

---

[7] In practice, the Desk limited the total amount of outright security holdings to maintain a "structural deficiency" in reserves; that is, permanent additions to reserves left supply short of the total that banks needed. The Desk's fine-tuning operations thus were primarily repos that temporarily boosted reserves.

[8] In a repo transaction, the Desk purchases a security from a designated primary dealer with an agreement to sell the security back to the dealer for a specified price at an agreed-upon date in the future. The term of the repo is the time between the Desk's purchase and the dealer's subsequent repurchase, which can be one day (overnight) or longer. The difference between the purchase price and the (usually higher) repurchase price, adjusted for the term of the repo, implies an interest rate for the repo. Because the Desk provides cash to the dealer in return for collateral, a repo is economically similar to a collateralized loan from the Desk to the dealer for the term of the repo. An RRP is the reverse of a repo transaction, with the Desk temporarily selling securities and the primary dealer or another counterparty providing cash. Thus, a repo serves to *increase* reserves, since the Desk temporarily purchases securities, while an RRP *reduces* reserves, because the counterparty's cash payment to the Federal Reserve is made by debiting the reserve account of the bank that clears the counterparty's trade.

[9] In particular, the FOMC's "Policy Normalization Principles and Plans" state that "[T]he Committee intends to reduce the Federal Reserve's securities holdings in a gradual and predictable manner primarily by ceasing to reinvest repayments of principal on securities held…" (FOMC 2014c). See further discussion of the FOMC's normalization principles in section 2.5.

2.3. Introduction of interest on excess reserves (IOER) in 2008

Prior to the financial crisis, reserve balances at the Federal Reserve did not earn interest. However, legislation passed in 2006 and 2008 authorized the Federal Reserve to pay interest on reserves held by depository institutions, starting in October 2008.[10] In the current environment in which the supply of reserves far exceeds the amount needed for reserve requirements, IOER—which is currently set at ¼ percent, or 25 basis points—has become the primary tool for keeping the overnight FFR within its target range of zero to ¼ percent.[11]

Excess reserves are effectively free of default and liquidity risk, so the IOER rate should be a lower bound for a bank's opportunity cost of alternative investments, such as loans or purchases of securities. Accordingly, if banks were the only investors (lenders) in money markets, IOER would set a floor for money market rates, as no bank would want to lend at a lower short-term interest rate.

To be sure, IOER is not available to many large and active money market investors, such as money market funds (MMFs), other cash-management vehicles, nonfinancial corporations, and government-sponsored enterprises (GSEs). But even though these investors cannot directly earn IOER, competition might be expected to lift money market rates up to (or close to) the level of the IOER rate, since banks—in the absence of frictions—should be able to earn an arbitrage profit on any funds that they borrow at a lower rate and then deposit at the Federal Reserve. Thus, in theory and without frictions, the IOER rate might still form a floor for short-term interest rates, allowing the Federal Reserve to achieve its target for the FFR even with a very high level of reserve balances.

In practice, however, the arbitrage across money market rates that could make the IOER rate effective as a floor on short-term rates is not costless. To undertake these actions, banks must expand their balance sheets to finance increased reserves, and banks face costs in doing so. For example, domestic banks are assessed Federal Deposit Insurance Corporation (FDIC) fees based on their total assets less tangible equity, and larger balance sheets also increase banks' capital and liquidity requirements and associated costs. Moreover, these costs are likely to rise with the implementation of new requirements for capital, particularly the Basel Committee on Banking Supervision's Basel III leverage ratio and the Federal Reserve's rules mandating that foreign banking organizations with large U.S. operations establish Intermediate Holding Companies (IHCs). These costs drive a wedge between the IOER rate earned by banks and the money

---

[10] The Financial Services Regulatory Relief Act of 2006 authorized interest payments on reserves beginning in 2011, and the Emergency Economic Stabilization Act of 2008 advanced the effective date of this authority to October 2008. The Federal Reserve pays interest on both required and excess reserves. These rates are currently the same, although they could be set at different levels. We focus on IOER because most reserves are excess reserves, so interest on excess reserves is more economically significant than that paid on required reserves.

[11] That is, under the current configuration of supply and demand for reserves—with supply far exceeding demand for required reserves—the operating framework to implement policy resembles a "floor system," rather than a corridor system (see note 4). In a floor system, a policy rate set by the central bank is intended to set a floor on other short-term rates. In practice, however, as discussed below, the IOER rate alone currently does not set a firm floor on short-term rates.

market rates that banks are willing to pay to finance reserves. As a result, the IOER rate does not set a firm floor under money market rates. Chart 1 shows the IOER rate and three money market rates: the FFR, the overnight GCF Treasury repo rate, and the overnight rate on AA-rated nonfinancial commercial paper (CP).[12] The three money market rates generally fall below IOER.

The gap between IOER and other rates probably reflects other factors, as well. For example, because IOER is available only to depository institutions, many active investors in money markets, such as MMFs and GSEs, may have limited bargaining power when providing the short-term funding that allows banks to arbitrage the IOER rate. Because MMFs generally only lend to institutions with top short-term credit ratings, the limited number of banks with such ratings may further increase their market power and widen the spread between IOER and other market rates. At the same time, the proximity of short-term interest rates to the zero lower bound, and structural features of the money markets that impede nominal interest rates from falling below zero, may be helping to keep the spread between IOER and money market rates relatively narrow.[13]

2.4. ON RRPs could complement IOER by helping to set a floor on short-term rates

One means of strengthening a floor for short-term interest rates would be to offer an overnight, risk-free instrument directly to a wider range of market participants. In July 2013, the Desk reported to the FOMC on the potential for such offerings in the form of fixed-rate, full-allotment ON RRPs, which could complement IOER in controlling short-term interest rates (FOMC 2013a). An RRP transaction is economically similar to the Federal Reserve borrowing from a counterparty, with the loan secured by collateral from the Federal Reserve's securities portfolio.[14] Thus, reserves and ON RRPs are both very short-term loans to the Federal Reserve, although reserves are unsecured and ON RRPs are secured. Like the IOER rate, the ON RRP rate (the rate of interest implied on an ON RRP transaction) is a risk-free rate of interest set by the Federal Reserve. However, while IOER is available only to depository institutions, ON RRPs can be made available to nonbank investors that are active in money markets.

Historically, the Federal Reserve conducted RRP (and repo) operations with primary dealer counterparties. However, in 2009, in anticipation of the potential need for large-scale RRPs, the

---

[12] The GCF (general collateral finance) Treasury repo rate is an index of rates on repos collateralized with Treasury securities. The index is published by the Depository Trust & Clearing Corporation (DTCC).

[13] Once the lower end of the FOMC's target range for the FFR is raised above zero, any role for the zero lower bound in narrowing spreads between the IOER rate and money market rates is likely to diminish. As such, the need for tools to establish a floor on short-term interest rates may become more apparent during policy normalization. This point is discussed in section 5.

[14] ON RRP transactions are structured as tri-party repos. To date, ON RRP transactions have been collateralized exclusively with Treasury securities.

Desk began to expand its set of counterparties for RRP operations. The Federal Reserve currently has 164 RRP counterparties, including primary dealers, banks, MMFs, and GSEs.[15]

In theory, as with the IOER rate, the ON RRP rate set by the FOMC would be expected to establish a floor on short-term interest rates, particularly if ON RRPs are available in sufficient quantity to satisfy demand at the ON RRP rate. Thus, the Desk's July 2013 presentation on the use of ON RRPs focused on a "fixed-rate, full-allotment" facility—that is, one that would offer ON RRPs without limit at the fixed rate set by the FOMC.[16] With such a facility in place, ON RRPs would always be available to counterparties as an alternative to other investments, so counterparties that can invest in ON RRPs generally should be unwilling to lend elsewhere at lower rates.

Since RRPs are accessible to a broad set of counterparties, including nonbank institutions that are significant money market lenders, access to ON RRPs should increase competitiveness in money markets and strengthen the effectiveness of the floor on rates. Whereas the effectiveness of a floor set by the IOER rate alone would depend on banks borrowing from money market investors at rates that are likely to be below the IOER rate, money market investors with access to ON RRP can lend directly to the Federal Reserve and earn the ON RRP rate. The option to invest in ON RRPs also would provide bargaining power to investors in their negotiations with borrowers in money markets, so even if actual ON RRP take-up is not very large, such a facility would help provide a floor on short-term interest rates and thus could be an important supplement to IOER in controlling the FFR.[17]

2.5. Tests of limited ON RRP offerings

In September 2013, the FOMC authorized the Desk to begin testing the use of ON RRPs as part of "an ongoing effort to improve the technical execution of policy" (FOMC 2013b).[18] The initial authorization set a range for the ON RRP rate of zero to 5 basis points and included a $1 billion cap on each individual counterparty's investments in ON RRP on each day. As shown in the table below, the actual individual-counterparty cap was initially set at $500 million, raised to $1 billion within a few days, and gradually increased to $10 billion over the next seven months. During this testing period, a fixed interest rate for ON RRPs was set on any given day, but that rate was moved over time in a range between 1 and 5 basis points for testing purposes.

---

[15] This total includes 25 new RRP counterparties that were added effective January 16, 2015 (see www.newyorkfed.org/markets/ec-150116.html). For a current list of RRP counterparties, see: www.ny.frb.org/markets/expanded_counterparties.html.

[16] In practice, the Federal Reserve's holdings of securities that can be used for ON RRP collateral place one constraint on aggregate take-up.

[17] As noted above, RRP transactions historically were used to drain reserves. Thus, RRP operations also could be used to help reduce excess reserves and make pre-crisis tools effective again for controlling the FFR. However, with the supply of reserves expected to remain very large for an extended period, the primary function of RRPs in the near term would be to assist IOER in setting a floor on short-term interest rates.

[18] The Desk's announcement of this testing exercise noted that the work was "a matter of prudent advance planning by the Federal Reserve" and that the "operations do not represent a change in the stance of monetary policy" (Federal Reserve Bank of New York 2013).

In September 2014, the FOMC directed to Desk to raise the individual-counterparty cap for the testing exercise to $30 billion and simultaneously introduced a $300 billion overall limit on the amount of ON RRPs that the Desk could offer each day (FOMC 2014d).[19] The FOMC also directed the Desk to use an auction process to set the interest rate on ON RRPs and allocate them among counterparties in the event that the overall limit is binding. Hence, under this phase of the exercise, the ON RRP rate is not always the "offering rate" set by the FOMC; when the overall limit is binding, the ON RRP rate set by the auction may be lower than the offering rate. (These testing features of the ON RRP exercise are described in further detail in section 4 below.)

Table. Timeline of the ON RRP exercise

September 2013	FOMC authorizes an ON RRP exercise through January 29, 2014, sets a range for the ON RRP offering rate of zero to 5 basis points, and puts a $1 billion cap on each individual counterparty's investments. Testing begins on September 23 with the per-counterparty cap set at $500 million, and it is raised a few days later to $1 billion.
December 2013	Cap on individual counterparties' investments raised to $3 billion.
January 2014	Authorization for ON RRP exercise is extended through January 2015, and cap on individual counterparties' investments is raised to $5 billion.[20]
March 2014	Cap on individual counterparties' investments raised to $7 billion.
April 2014	Cap on individual counterparties' investments raised to $10 billion.
September 2014	FOMC sets a $300 billion overall limit on the amount of ON RRP that can be offered each day, raises the cap on individual counterparties' investments to $30 billion, and introduces an auction process to allocate ON RRPs (and set an interest rate) in the event that the overall limit is binding.
October 2014	FOMC authorizes testing of modest, temporary adjustments of the ON RRP offering rate to as high as 10 basis points.
December 2014	Authorization for ON RRP exercise is extended through January 2016, and $300 billion in *term* RRPs spanning year-end are offered in a series of four auctions.
January 2015	FOMC authorizes up to $50 billion in term RRP operations in February and early March, and $200 billion of term RRP operations that span the March 2015 quarter-end.

Also in September 2014, the FOMC published a statement on its Policy Normalization Principles and Plans, which indicated that the FFR will continue to play a central role in monetary policy

---

[19] As noted in the September 2014 FOMC Minutes, "Testing these design features was generally seen as furthering the Committee's understanding of how an ON RRP facility might be structured to best balance its objectives of supporting monetary control and of limiting the Federal Reserve's role in financial intermediation as well as reducing potential financial stability risks the facility might pose during periods of stress" (FOMC 2014d).

[20] The authorization approved by the Committee at its January 2014 meeting did not specify a particular level for the per-counterparty cap, but stipulated that any change to this cap would require approval by the Chairman.

implementation during normalization (FOMC 2014c). The statement noted that "[w]hen economic conditions and the economic outlook warrant a less accommodative monetary policy, the Committee will raise its target range for the federal funds rate," and "the Federal Reserve intends to move the federal funds rate into the target range set by the FOMC primarily by adjusting the interest rate it pays on excess reserve balances." The FOMC also stated:

> During normalization, the Federal Reserve intends to use an overnight reverse repurchase agreement facility and other supplementary tools as needed to help control the federal funds rate. The Committee will use an overnight reverse repurchase agreement facility only to the extent necessary and will phase it out when it is no longer needed to help control the federal funds rate (FOMC 2014c).

ON RRP testing has also included temporary changes in the ON RRP offering rate. As noted above, that rate varied between 1 and 5 basis points for the first several months of the exercise. In October 2014, the FOMC authorized testing of ON RRP rates between 0 and 10 basis points. The offering rate was lowered to 3 basis points in early November, then raised to 7 basis points in mid-November and to 10 basis points in early December, and finally returned to 5 basis points in mid-December.

Another potential supplementary tool that is closely related to ON RRPs is *term* RRPs, that is, reverse repos for which the sale of securities and their repurchase occur more than one business day apart.[21] In October 2014, the FOMC instructed the Desk to offer up to $300 billion in term RRP operations with the same set of counterparties used for ON RRP operations. The operations were intended to test term RRPs "as a supplementary tool to help control the federal funds rate, particularly when there are significant and transitory shifts in money market activity." In particular, the FOMC instructed the Desk to conduct term RRP operations that would cross year-end 2014—that is, to sell securities before year-end and repurchase them in the first few days of January 2015 (Federal Reserve Bank of New York 2014b). As described below, money-market rates historically have exhibited significant variation at quarter- and year-ends, so the year-end was a useful period in which to assess the ability of RRPs—both term and overnight—to help control short-term rates. Over the last four weeks of December 2014, the Desk conducted four term RRP operations that offered a total of $300 billion in term RRPs, all of which matured on January 5, 2015.[22]

The Federal Reserve continues to enhance operational readiness and increase its understanding of the impact of RRPs through technical exercises. For example, in January 2015, the FOMC authorized up to $50 billion in term RRP operations for February and early March, and $200 billion of term RRP operations that would span the March 2015 quarter-end (Federal Reserve Bank of New York 2015).

---

[21] In contrast, as noted above, for *overnight* RRP, the sale and repurchase occur on successive business days. The Desk had previously conducted small-scale tests of term RRPs, largely to ensure that this tool would be ready if the FOMC decided to use it to drain reserves.

[22] As noted in section 2.6, total take-up from these four term RRP auctions was $226 billion.

2.6. Results of ON RRP testing to date

Testing to date suggests that the ON RRP exercise, even in limited size, has helped control short-term interest rates. Chart 2 adds the ON RRP offering rate to chart 1 to show that this rate generally has served as an effective floor on short-term interest rates since the beginning of the ON RRP exercise. On most days, for example, the Treasury GCF rate has remained above the ON RRP rate.

Chart 3 illustrates counterparties' take-up of ON RRPs. In first three months of the ON RRP exercise, from September to December 2013, when the cap on each counterparty's usage was at most $1 billion, aggregate take-up averaged only $8 billion. ON RRP usage subsequently rose, in part reflecting increases in the counterparty cap. From April 7 to September 19, 2014, when the individual counterparty cap was $10 billion, aggregate take-up averaged $140 billion. Since September 22, 2014, the individual cap has been $30 billion, and usage has averaged $131 billion.[23]

The chart also shows the composition of counterparties' participation in the ON RRP exercise. MMFs generally account for most of the take-up; since April 7, 2014, MMF usage has averaged $116 billion, or 85 percent of average aggregate take-up.

As shown in chart 4, ON RRP take-up generally increases when the spread between market rates—in this case, the overnight GCF Treasury repo rate—and the ON RRP rate narrows. That is, ON RRP demand rises when the ON RRP rate is higher relative to market interest rates on other short-term investments.

As chart 3 illustrates, ON RRP take-up has spiked at recent quarter-ends, largely because borrower demand for short-term funding drops sharply on those dates. Much of this drop-off in demand reflects so-called "window dressing" by financial institutions. For example, foreign banking organizations trim borrowing at quarter-ends to reduce the size of their balance sheets, since bank capital regulations in some countries are based on assets measured at the end of each quarter. Hence, MMFs and other cash investors, facing reduced opportunities to invest at quarter-ends, have shifted money into ON RRP. Take-up has jumped at the end of each quarter since the testing exercise began, and usage reached a record $339 billion at the end of June 2014. Demand was even higher, at $407 billion, on September 30, 2014, but with the $300 billion overall limit in place, only that lower amount of ON RRP was awarded to counterparties, and the auction process was used to allocate ON RRP among them. This auction procedure (described in more detail in section 4) caused the rate paid on ON RRPs (the "stop-out rate") to fall to 0 basis points that day.

The limited availability of ON RRPs on the quarter-end date of September 30, 2014, apparently contributed to a drop in the Treasury GCF rate below the ON RRP offering rate on two days in late September as well as on the quarter-end day itself. As shown in chart 2, on September 30,

---

[23] Offerings of term RRPs in December 2014 likely contributed to a decline in average ON RRP use in that month. Total RRP usage, including both ON and term RRPs, has averaged $156 billion since September 22, 2014.

the Treasury GCF rate fell to 1.8 basis points, its lowest level of the year. The decline in rates on days prior to September 30 reportedly reflected money market investors' expectations that the overall limit would be binding on that day and their efforts to invest in substitute assets beforehand.[24]

Chart 2 also shows that, in contrast to the drop in money-market rates that occurred at the end of September 2014, short-term interest rates generally stayed above the ON RRP offering rate at the end of December. That result likely reflected, at least in part, the offerings of term RRPs that spanned year-end 2014, which augmented the available supply of RRPs with the Federal Reserve. That is, at year-end, total Federal Reserve offerings of RRPs reached $600 billion: $300 billion in ON RRPs and $300 billion in term RRPs. Total RRP take-up on December 31 was $397 billion—$171 billion in ON RRPs and $226 billion in term RRPs—just short of the $407 billion in bids submitted on September 30 for ON RRPs.

3. Some potential secondary effects of an ON RRP facility

An ON RRP facility is a monetary policy tool that could play an important role in controlling interest rates during the normalization process, and a full-allotment facility that places no limits on ON RRP offerings might be especially effective in this regard. At the same time, a facility that offers ON RRP in very large amounts, even if it were not full-allotment, could have some significant secondary effects, including impacts on short-term funding market structure and financial stability. Policymakers, academics, and market observers have identified several potential consequences with both positive and negative implications, and this section describes those possibilities in detail. We follow up this section with analysis, in section 4, of some potential features in the design of an ON RRP facility that might mitigate or prevent secondary effects that could be undesirable.

One implication of a very large ON RRP facility would be the expansion of the Federal Reserve's intermediation in short-term funding markets, which—particularly if such a facility were permanently in place—could alter financial markets in unpredictable ways. Concerns about a larger Federal Reserve footprint in short-term funding markets were raised at the June 2014 FOMC meeting, at which "a number of participants noted that a relatively large ON RRP facility had the potential to expand the Federal Reserve's role in financial intermediation and reshape the financial industry in ways that were difficult to anticipate" (FOMC 2014a).

The presence of an ON RRP facility also could have implications for financial stability. A potentially beneficial effect arises from the provision of a very safe, short-term asset. A recent academic literature suggests that official-sector issuance of debt instruments with money-like characteristics can displace private short-term assets that are prone to runs.[25] Thus, by supplying

---

[24] The Federal Reserve's September 17, 2014 announcement of changes to the ON RRP exercise, including the introduction of the $300 billion overall limit, came shortly before the end of the quarter (Federal Reserve Bank of New York 2014a). A subsequent scramble among investors for money market assets late in the quarter may have contributed to the decline in rates.

[25] As described below, this literature includes Stein (2012); Greenwood, Hanson, and Stein (2013); Krishnamurthy and Vissing-Jorgensen (2013); and Carlson et al. (2014).

ON RRPs with money-like features, the facility might mitigate some risks to financial stability, although this effect would be incidental to the facility's primary purpose.

However, a facility that could allow a very rapid and unexpected expansion of ON RRP might exacerbate disruptive flight-to-quality flows during a period of financial stress and thus could undermine financial stability. Market observers and policymakers both have described such risks. For example, the Minutes of the June 2014 FOMC meeting state that "[m]ost participants expressed concerns that in times of financial stress, the facility's counterparties could shift investments toward the facility and away from financial and nonfinancial corporations, possibly causing disruptions in funding that could magnify the stress" (FOMC 2014a).

The extent of the potential secondary effects of an ON RRP facility likely would depend on both the size of the facility and its potential rate of expansion. The possibility of unpredictable effects arising from a larger Federal Reserve footprint in short-term funding markets, as well as the potential benefits of supplying safe money-like assets, would be associated with the *level* of facility usage. In contrast, as described below, the risk of exacerbating a disruptive flight to quality would be more closely linked to the potential for facility usage to significantly *increase* suddenly and unexpectedly. Below, we examine these possible secondary effects in greater detail.

3.1. Potential effects of a very large ON RRP facility on financial intermediation

By offering a new form of overnight risk-free investment, an ON RRP facility could attract cash from investors who otherwise might provide funding for private institutions and firms. That is, the facility could expand the Federal Reserve's role in financial markets by offering investors a new tool to manage liquidity and thus could crowd out some private financing. Such crowding out may have both desirable and undesirable consequences: This section describes some potential adverse implications, while section 3.2 describes some possible benefits.

Some crowding out of short-term funding is likely during any monetary-tightening phase, as short-term interest rates rise and some borrowers that have obtained funding at low rates are unwilling to pay higher rates. Since the purpose of an ON RRP facility is to help set a floor for short-term interest rates by offering investors an alternative risk-free asset, an ON RRP facility should be expected to supplant some private financing activity, particularly when the FOMC decides to raise the target range for the FFR.

Importantly, increased ON RRP take-up does not expand the size of the Federal Reserve's balance sheet or the volume of private short-term funding required to finance that balance sheet. Instead, such an increase shifts the *composition* of the Federal Reserve's liabilities from reserves held by banks to RRPs that can be held by a wider range of institutions. Hence, the crowding out of private financing that results from greater use of ON RRP would largely represent a reduction in private lending by money-market investors to banks that are financing reserves, offset by an increase in private lending by those investors directly to the Federal Reserve. Given the IOER and ON RRP rates that are set by the Federal Reserve, the allocation of Federal Reserve liabilities between reserves and RRPs is ultimately determined in markets.

Nonetheless, the resulting crowding out of private short-term financing may have some adverse implications. Most importantly, a permanently expanded role for the Federal Reserve in short-term funding markets could reshape the financial industry in ways that may be difficult to anticipate and that may prove to be undesirable. For example, a permanent or long-lasting facility that causes very significant crowding out of short-term financing could lead to atrophying of the private infrastructure that supports these markets. Partially in response to some of these concerns, the FOMC has made clear that an ON RRP facility is not intended to be permanent (FOMC 2014c).

The amount of short-term financing that could be crowded out would depend largely on the elasticity of demand for private financing—that is, the extent to which private firms are willing to raise rates that they pay for short-term funding to remain competitive with a new risk-free asset. The limited testing of ON RRPs to date suggests that the amounts in question could be substantial relative to the size of the market for Treasury tri-party repo but still only a small fraction of overall volumes in money markets. As noted in section 2, since September 22, 2014, when the individual-counterparty cap was raised to $30 billion, ON RRP take-up has averaged $131 billion. During the same period, total tri-party repo against Treasury securities collateral averaged $667 billion, and repo against all U.S. government securities collateral averaged $1.26 trillion, although tri-party repo represents only a fraction of outstanding money market instruments in which ON RRP counterparties invest cash.[26] We are not aware of any evidence that the testing of the facility to date has affected the structure of the money market.

Chart 5 suggests that ON RRPs have served as a substitute for some private financing, although recent declines in private short-term funding probably have reflected factors other than the availability of ON RRPs. The chart shows volumes of repo backed by U.S. government securities ("government repo") held by MMFs. As the chart indicates, MMFs' private financing through government repo was declining before ON RRP became available, at least in part because of pressures on financial institutions to trim their balance sheets in light of new regulatory requirements for capital.[27] The chart shows that increasing ON RRP take-up since testing operations began in September 2013 has offset a fairly steep decline in government repo financing for private entities. So, in this case, increased ON RRP take-up may reflect in part the deleveraging of financial institutions, rather than the crowding out of private short-term financing.

3.2. Potential effects of an ON RRP facility on financial stability

In principle, there are two distinct channels through which the establishment of an ON RRP facility could affect financial stability. First, the availability of an elastically supplied risk-free asset could influence the likelihood that money market investors would shift rapidly from providing private short-term funding to holding only very safe assets. That is, the facility could

---

[26] These figures include ON RRP transactions.

[27] The requirements include the Basel III leverage ratio introduced by the Basel Committee on Banking Supervision in 2010, which was implemented in the U.S. through the supplementary leverage ratio in 2013, as well as Federal Reserve rules adopted in 2014 that require foreign banking organizations with large U.S. operations to establish U.S. intermediate holding companies (IHCs) that generally will be subject to the same capital standards applicable to U.S. bank holding companies.

affect the chance of a widespread run. Second, an ON RRP facility could affect the dynamics and severity of such a shift, once it is under way.

The academic literature does not provide strong guidance regarding the effects of a new risk-free asset on the likelihood of sudden shifts toward safe assets. On the one hand, a recent literature has emphasized the benefits of the public provision of safe short-term assets, such as ON RRPs, in enhancing financial stability by displacing private money-like assets that are prone to runs. On the other hand, some models suggest that the availability of an attractive safe investment could increase the likelihood of runs.

However, once a run is underway, the availability of ON RRPs could allow greater flight-to-quality flows during a run and thus could exacerbate the run and its effects. These effects might be particularly significant with a full-allotment ON RRP facility, but they also could occur with facility that does not offer full allotment if its structure leaves the potential for a sudden and unexpected large increase in take-up.

3.2.1. Effect on the likelihood of runs

The academic literature has not directly considered the broad effects of introducing an elastically supplied risk-free asset, and the insights that can be gained from existing models are somewhat limited, in part because these models do not deliver robust predictions. Hence, the literature overall does not provide clear-cut predictions about how an ON RRP facility would affect the likelihood of a run.

A recent literature has suggested that the provision of short-term safe assets by the official sector could enhance financial stability by displacing private money-like liquid assets and reducing the risk of runs (Stein 2012; Greenwood, Hanson, and Stein 2013; Krishnamurthy and Vissing-Jorgensen 2013; Carlson et al. 2014). Gorton and Metrick (2012) have argued that private issuance of money-like assets, particularly before the financial crisis, was a response to a shortage of safe short-term instruments, and that these private instruments can leave issuers vulnerable to runs. Stein (2012) and Greenwood, Hanson, and Stein (2013) state that increasing the supply of safe short-term assets may be more effective than regulatory responses to the externalities associated with private money-like assets, especially those created by the shadow-banking sector.

In principle, the benefits of displacing private money-like instruments could be realized either with an increase in government liabilities, such as Treasury bills, which can be held by a wide range of investors, or an increase in central bank liabilities, such as ON RRPs, that are available to large and active money market investors. Government creation of short-term safe assets via increased issuance of short-term instruments has some drawbacks, however, such as greater rollover risk to the government (see, for example, Greenwood, Hanson, and Stein 2013). This concern is less relevant for ON RRPs, since a reduction in investor demand for ON RRPs would simply result in an offsetting rise in reserves.

Models in the tradition of Diamond and Dybvig (1983) consider the fragility of a financial institution that must choose between a short-term safe asset (like an investment in an ON RRP facility), and a long-term technology. In these models, an exogenous increase in the return on the safe asset, analogous to an increase in the ON RRP rate, has both a substitution and an income effect. The substitution effect reflects the tendency to increase investment in the safe asset as its higher return makes it more desirable. The income effect reflects the opposite tendency—to reduce investment in the asset because one can earn the same income with a lower quantity of the asset. In principle, either effect could dominate.[28] Increasing the return on the safe asset could reduce the range of parameter values for which the financial institution is vulnerable to runs, but there are no general results establishing the conditions under which such an effect could occur.[29]

Another relevant theoretical result is that, by giving investors an attractive outside option (a safe asset supplied elastically at a fixed rate), an ON RRP facility could increase the likelihood of a run. This result occurs, for example, in some game theoretic models (see, for example, Morris and Shin 2010). However, these models do not consider possible endogenous reactions that could offset the increased risk. For example, borrowers who rely on funding from lenders that are more likely to run because of access to an ON RRP facility could reduce this risk by increasing the term of their funding.

3.2.2. Effect on the dynamics and severity of a run (once it is underway)

Absent an ON RRP facility, in the event of a widespread run from private short-term funding markets, the supply of safe assets, such as Treasury securities, would not expand automatically to accommodate increased demand.[30] Hence, without ON RRPs, opportunities to run may be constrained by a limited supply of risk-free assets, and greater demand for those assets is likely to push up their prices and make running more costly.

By contrast, an ON RRP facility that elastically supplies a very safe asset and which has the potential to increase in size by very large amounts would provide no immediate mechanism to slow a run. Hence, some market observers have suggested that such a facility could exacerbate flight-to-quality flows and their repercussions (Wrightson ICAP 2014). In section 4, we describe some possible ON RRP facility design features, such as caps on usage, that could address these concerns. Here, however, we focus on the possible effects of a facility without such features.

To be sure, an ON RRP facility may have some benefits during a run. By displacing private money-like assets prior to the run, ON RRPs might dampen the run and ameliorate some of the damage it causes. Moreover, the availability of ON RRPs could diminish the incentive to run to safe assets, such as Treasury securities or MMFs that hold only U.S. government securities.

---

[28] For example, if a depositor's utility function displays constant relative risk aversion, then whether the substitution or the income effect dominates depends on the degree of risk aversion.

[29] For example, Ennis and Keister (2006) provide a sufficient condition for a bank to be run-proof that depends on the return of the safe asset.

[30] Safe-haven flows may be limited by other constraints, as well. For example, MMFs that invest exclusively in Treasury and other U.S. government securities have at times stopped accepting new investments, especially when heightened demand for those securities pushed their interest rates down to very low levels.

Because the prices of safe assets tend to rise in such scenarios, and government-only MMFs can close their doors to new investors, there may be an incentive to front-run other investors. An ON RRP facility that elastically supplies a safe asset at a fixed rate could diminish this incentive.[31]

In the next two sections, we consider some recent flights to quality and discuss how an ON RRP facility might affect financial stability during such an event.

3.2.3. The dynamics of some recent widespread flights to quality

Short-term funding markets historically have been buffeted by sudden flights to safety, when investors have abruptly sought to limit risk exposure by switching quickly from risky assets to safer ones. Prior to the introduction of deposit insurance, these episodes typically involved widespread bank runs. The emergence of a large wholesale funding market in the United States in recent decades has set the stage for large-scale runs on the liabilities and shares of nonbank issuers, such as the runs on MMFs, repo, and CP that occurred in 2007-2008.

To illustrate the types and magnitudes of the rapid shifts that have occurred in short-term funding markets during flights to quality, we examine a recent episode of financial strain: September 2008, when the most precipitous runs of the 2007-2009 crisis occurred. (An appendix examines two additional episodes of more modest flight-to-quality flows that occurred during the debt-ceiling standoffs of 2011 and 2013.) We focus primarily on flows that occurred during a *one-week* window, to highlight the types of flows that may present the greatest threats to financial stability.

Of course, flight-to-quality dynamics during future crises are likely to be quite different from those in past episodes. For example, the 2008 crisis was an unusually large shock—not a typical flight-to-quality episode—although the flows that occurred during that crisis probably would have been significantly larger without government interventions, including the Federal Reserve's liquidity programs and actions by the Treasury and FDIC. In addition, legal, regulatory, and other changes since 2008 will probably affect the nature and scale of future flight-to-quality episodes. For example, new regulations that require banks to hold larger liquid-asset buffers than in 2008, as well as the large amount of reserves currently in the banking system, may ameliorate some of the effects of large-scale runs on short-term funding instruments. Still, recent flights to quality can provide a sense of the magnitudes of flow that could create financial stability concerns.

How large were flows to safe havens in September 2008?

The most severe flight-to-quality flows in 2008 occurred in the week of September 15-19, when the Lehman bankruptcy caused losses at prime MMFs and the Reserve Primary Fund "broke the buck." A variety of safe havens attracted inflows, including government MMFs and bank liquid deposits.[32] As shown in chart 6, government MMF assets increased $190 billion between

---

[31] This type of effect is studied, in a different context, in Cipriani, Martin, McCabe, and Parigi (2014).

[32] For many safe assets, such as Treasury bills, supply did not increase over the week (Treasury bill supply actually declined during the week of September 15-19, so *net* flows were negative), and the marked increase in demand

September 12 and 19, and bank liquid deposits increased $100 billion.[33] The largest *daily* flight-to-quality flow that week—adding up inflows to government MMFs and liquid deposits—was $140 billion, on September 18.[34]

Where did investors run from in September 2008?

During the 2007-2008 crisis, investors ran from virtually every short-term vehicle that embedded liquidity and credit risk, although the timing and severity of runs on individual instruments varied considerably.[35] Chart 6 shows that in the week of September 15-19, 2008, investors redeemed $310 billion, on net, from prime MMFs. Investors also ran from other short-term funding instruments; for example, CP outstanding dropped $110 billion that week.

As MMFs came under redemption pressure, they contributed to the pullback from risky assets. Prime MMFs' holdings of CP and repo dropped $150 billion and $70 billion, respectively, between September 9 and 23, while holdings of Treasury securities declined just $7 billion and time deposits held about steady.[36] Notably, much of the redemption pressure on prime MMFs was alleviated when the Treasury announced its temporary guarantee program for MMFs on September 19, as the run on MMFs subsequently slowed significantly. In addition, the Federal Reserve's Asset-Backed Commercial Paper Money Market Mutual Fund Liquidity Facility (AMLF), which ultimately facilitated MMFs' sales (at no loss to them) of $150 billion in asset-backed CP to banking organizations, and the Primary Dealer Credit Facility (PDCF), also probably dampened flight-to-quality flows.[37]

An important lesson from recent crises is that sudden changes in the perception of the relative risk of various investments may lead to sharp differences in flow patterns. For example, in late 2007 and early 2008, prime MMFs were apparently viewed as safer than some near substitutes, such as enhanced-cash funds and other private liquidity funds, and prime MMF assets increased $350 billion from August 2007 to August 2008. Of course, the direction of flows changed dramatically amid the run in September 2008. The appendix, which examines other episodes of

---

resulted in higher prices and lower yields. Yields on 4-week and 3-month Treasury bills dropped from about 150 basis points on September 11 to under 10 basis points on September 17.

[33] Liquid deposits include transaction accounts and savings deposits at weekly FR 2900 reporters, which comprise about 2500 institutions, including the largest domestic banks in terms of reservable liabilities and M2 deposits (liquid deposits plus small time deposits), as well as all foreign banking organizations.

[34] Some of these flows may have been impeded by quantity restrictions, such as MMF closures to new investments, although available data do not provide information on their use in September 2008.

[35] For example, between August 2007 and October 2008, investors sharply curtailed funding for asset-backed commercial paper, auction-rate securities, tender-option bonds, securities-lending cash collateral investment pools, enhanced-cash and other private liquidity funds, repo, deposits at certain banks, prime MMFs, offshore MMFs, and bank short-term investment trusts. Runs on different instruments did not necessarily occur simultaneously; for example, in late 2007 and early 2008, when some private liquidity funds were experiencing runs, prime MMFs were attracting large inflows.

[36] Based on data from iMoneyNet and authors' calculations. Note that the portfolio holdings of the Reserve Primary Fund are excluded from these figures, since that fund's assets were not reflected accurately in iMoneyNet data.

[37] For a description of the Federal Reserve's Credit and Liquidity Programs deployed during the crisis, see www.federalreserve.gov/monetarypolicy/bst_crisisresponse.htm.

stress, provides additional examples of how the *direction* of flight-to-quality flows may differ from one episode to the next.

3.2.4. How might a potentially large ON RRP facility alter flight-to-quality dynamics?

As noted above, an ON RRP facility could have some beneficial effects during a run. It could diminish incentives to move cash to safe assets ahead of other investors if there is certainty about access during periods of stress. Furthermore, if the facility is large enough to have displaced a significant fraction of private money-like assets before a run begins, the facility could dampen the scale of a run and mitigate the damage it causes.

However, an elastically supplied risk-free asset also could amplify run dynamics, such as those that have occurred in past flight-to-quality episodes, and alter the destinations of safe-haven flows. Cash that, in the absence of ON RRPs, might have moved quickly to liquid deposits at banks could go instead into a risk-free ON RRP facility through, for example, government MMFs that invest in ON RRPs. The sources of flight-to-quality flows, such as prime MMFs, could experience larger outflows than in past episodes, and the availability of short-term funding for broker-dealer and nonfinancial firms through vehicles like repo and CP could decline more quickly.

The safe-haven flows in previous stress episodes can provide a benchmark for the potential scale of flows that, at a time of heightened risk aversion, might be *redirected* to an ON RRP facility from financial institutions or funds that served as safe havens in past flights to quality. However, such flows tell us little about the potential *additional* flight-to-quality flows that might occur because an ON RRP facility has created a new, elastically supplied risk-free asset. Some potential mechanisms for incremental flows include greater within-portfolio shifts to safe assets by MMFs that are ON RRP counterparties, larger redemptions from prime MMFs and inflows to government MMFs that hold ON RRPs, and larger inflows to these government MMFs (or directly to an ON RRP facility) from other sources.

Outstanding amounts of short-dated money market instruments can illustrate the *potential* for large net flows to safe-haven destinations, such as an ON RRP facility, that can accommodate incoming cash. For example, the aggregate assets of institutional prime MMFs, which would be at risk of sudden, heavy redemptions in a crisis, suggest that such flows could be several hundred billion dollars.[38] To be clear, some such flows are likely in an episode of financial stress, regardless of the existence of an ON RRP facility, so the overall size of potential flight-to-quality flows cannot inform us about the marginal impact of an ON RRP facility on these flows. Still, the magnitudes in question indicate that flight-to-quality inflows to a facility could be very large.

---

[38] Institutional prime MMFs have proven to be particularly vulnerable to runs in past episodes of stress (see, for example, U.S. Securities and Exchange Commission 2013, pages 72-76).

What are the financial stability implications of the potential changes in flight-to-quality flows during crises?

The effects of changes in flight-to-safety flows on financial stability and economic activity would depend in large part on the nature of the institutions and firms that might lose short-term funding if investors shift to ON RRPs. Data on the short-term assets held by MMFs, which are very large investors in these markets, suggest that the institutions and firms in question would mostly be large banks—particularly foreign banks—and their subsidiaries, including broker-dealers (these data are discussed in the appendix). The ultimate recipients of this financing are less certain, but they could have included clients, such as hedge funds and nonfinancial firms, that normally obtain funding from the banks and broker-dealers. However, a substantial amount of the short-term borrowing, particularly by foreign banks, was likely used to finance IOER arbitrage, and the withdrawal of that portion of the short-term funding likely would not have any adverse effects on financial stability.

The redirection of cash that might have gone to liquid deposits in the past may also have stability implications. Banks that received such cash would have had a broader range of options for reinvesting it than the government MMFs that are likely to attract inflows because of their access to ON RRPs. In addition, Gatev, Schuermann, and Strahan (2009) argue that deposit inflows may have bolstered bank liquidity during past episodes of stress. However, regulatory changes discussed in section 2 are probably making large flight-to-quality deposit inflows, particularly those from institutional investors, less attractive for many banks.

To be sure, most surges in ON RRP take-up probably would have no bearing on financial stability. For example, seasonal reductions in the supply of Treasury bills may cause jumps in ON RRP usage that are unrelated to financial stability. Also, when private borrowers' *demand* for short-term funding drops—for example, as foreign banking organizations and some domestic banks trim borrowing at quarter-ends—investors may shift money into ON RRPs. The resulting increases in take-up are unlikely to be disruptive.

In fact, as noted in section 2, large one-day increases in ON RRP usage have already occurred on dates when borrower demand for short-term funding has dropped, particularly on quarter-end dates. Take-up jumped $199 billion and $131 billion on the last days of June and December 2014, respectively. Moreover, demand rose by $213 billion on the last day of September 2014, although the aggregate cap limited the increase in awards that day to $105 billion. Rather than being disruptive, these increases in ON RRP take-up so far appear to have smoothed the supply of money market assets, particularly at quarter-ends when borrowers' demand for short-term funding typically falls.

In contrast, the surges in usage that would be cause for concern would be those triggered by stress-related flights to quality, which presumably would be due to reductions in investors' (that is, lenders') willingness to *supply* short-term funding to private firms and institutions. The scale of one-day increases in ON RRP take-up indicates that money market participants, such as MMFs, have the potential to direct large flows quickly to ON RRPs.

Why does a large and unexpected increase in ON RRP take-up have financial stability implications during a flight to quality? Isn't provision of safe assets during crises one of the roles of the Federal Reserve?

Provision of safe assets to the financial system is a core central-bank function. Indeed, the official title of the Federal Reserve Act is "An Act to provide for the establishment of Federal reserve banks, to furnish an elastic currency…" Increasing the supply of ON RRP could in principle be seen as similar to classic means of furnishing an elastic currency, such as open market purchases or lender-of-last-resort functions like discount-window lending.

However, an increase in ON RRP, which absorbs cash from the private sector, has very different implications for the availability of liquidity and credit in the economy than the classic central-bank tools that augment liquidity in periods of stress. Those classic tools, such as lender-of-last-resort extensions of credit to banks through Discount Window loans, involve the Federal Reserve's provision of cash against less-liquid private assets that serve as collateral, and hence do not cause any reduction in available credit to private borrowers. For example, a private debt instrument that is pledged at the Discount Window in exchange for Federal Reserve liabilities (cash or reserves) remains intact. In contrast, all else equal, increased ON RRP usage implies reduced short-term financing for other borrowers. If, for example, MMFs quickly shift from investing in commercial paper or repo to holding ON RRPs, they would reduce the availability of short-term credit for private firms and institutions. More generally, in contrast to classic central-bank liquidity provision, which creates reserves, increased ON RRP take-up diminishes reserves.

The Federal Reserve could take actions to offset the reduction in available liquidity that might be caused by a flight-to-quality event, including a surge of inflows to an ON RRP facility. In particular, the Federal Reserve could use its traditional tools for injecting liquidity back into the financial system, such as providing funding through the Discount Window to commercial banks with liquidity shortfalls and providing liquidity broadly through repos backed by OMO-eligible securities with primary dealers. The Federal Reserve also could employ unconventional tools, such as large-scale asset purchases (LSAPs) of U.S. government securities and—subject to the provisions of the Dodd-Frank Act—establishing broad-based facilities under section 13(3) of the Federal Reserve Act to provide credit to a broad set of nonbank financial institutions and nonfinancial firms. Still, some limitations in these tools and in the Federal Reserve's ability to employ some of them expeditiously suggest some caution regarding the efficacy of a potential response to disruptive flight-to-quality flows.[39] For these and other reasons, it may be prudent to design an ON RRP facility with features that would mitigate the risk of sharp, potentially disruptive surges of ON RRP take-up, while preserving the facility's usefulness in helping to control short-term interest rates.

---

[39] For example, stigma associated with Discount Window borrowing may limit its effectiveness in providing liquidity, repos with dealer firms can be executed only against certain forms of high-quality collateral, and extending credit quickly to nonbank financial institutions and nonfinancial firms would be challenging.

4. Some options for ON RRP facility design features aimed at addressing potentially undesirable secondary effects

In this section, we discuss some possible design features and safeguards for an ON RRP facility that could address the potentially undesirable secondary effects that were discussed in section 3, while also providing the FOMC with the desired degree of control over the FFR. In particular, we discuss measures that could limit the role of the Federal Reserve in financial intermediation and constrain sudden, sharp increases in take-up that might threaten financial stability. These measures include making the ON RRP facility temporary, changes in the ON RRP rate, quantity controls, and combinations of rate changes and quantity controls. It is worth noting that a number of regulatory changes over recent years have been aimed at boosting the liquidity positions of financial institutions and reducing run risks in short-term funding markets. Consistent with the spirit of those regulations, the design features discussed in this section are aimed at minimizing any potential for ON RRP operations to exacerbate liquidity risks in short-term funding markets.

4.1. Making the ON RRP facility temporary

Making an ON RRP facility temporary would help to address concerns that such a facility could expand the Federal Reserve's role in financial intermediation and reshape the financial industry in ways that are difficult to anticipate and that may prove to be undesirable. A temporary facility is less likely than a permanent one to cause lenders to curtail relationships with money-market borrowers, to abandon money-market infrastructure, and to rely exclusively on ON RRPs as a place to invest cash. Indeed, market participants appear to be maintaining counterparty relationships, perhaps in part because they anticipate that the facility will be discontinued when it is no longer needed to support money market rates.

The FOMC has indicated that, although an ON RRP facility will be useful in controlling short-term rates during normalization, the Committee does not anticipate that such a facility will be a permanent part of the Committee's longer-run operating framework. As noted in the Policy Normalization Principles and Plans released in September 2014, the Committee will use an ON RRP facility only to the extent necessary and will phase it out when it is no longer needed to help control the FFR (FOMC 2014c).

Consistent with the expectation that an ON RRP facility would be temporary in nature, the Federal Reserve Bank of New York announced in November 2014 that it is unlikely to further modify the eligibility criteria for RRP counterparties. The Federal Reserve Bank of New York also noted that it did not anticipate increasing the total number of RRP counterparties after adding those from a wave of applications in late 2014 (Federal Reserve Bank of New York 2014c).

In addition, as indicated in the Policy Normalization Principles and Plans, the Committee intends to reduce its securities holdings in a gradual and predictable manner primarily by ceasing to reinvest repayments of principal. This process will result in a reduction in excess reserves, and thus gradually improve the extent to which IOER exerts upward pressure on money market rates. For example, a lower amount of reserves in the banking system should reduce banks' balance sheet costs and the costs associated with arbitrage activities, and hence foster a tighter link between the IOER and other market rates. In addition, reducing reserves should make them scarcer (at least for some banks), increase banks' competition for reserves, and facilitate tighter control of the FFR. Against this backdrop, when the FOMC is confident that the IOER rate—perhaps supported by supplementary tools other than an ON RRP facility—is exerting a sufficiently strong pull on money market rates, the ON RRP facility will no longer be needed.

The FOMC has other supplementary tools that could be used to hasten the phase-out of an ON RRP facility, if the Committee determines that doing so would be appropriate. For example, during the normalization process, the Committee could complement ON RRPs with term RRPs. The Federal Reserve could also use a Term Deposit Facility (TDF), which would allow banks to maintain term deposits with the Federal Reserve at a higher rate than the IOER rate. These tools could provide additional arbitrage opportunities for banks and nonbanks and help to exert upward pressures on money market rates. Furthermore, use of these tools would diminish the supply of reserves. Finally, the Committee could also choose to sell assets, which all else equal, would reduce the amount of reserves in the banking system and diminish the aggregate size of the banking system's balance sheet. As noted above, both of these effects would help to put upward pressure on short-term interest rates.

4.2. Setting the spread between the IOER rate and the ON RRP rate

Reducing the ON RRP offering rate to make investments in ON RRPs less attractive would be one way to address concerns that a relatively large ON RRP facility could expand the Federal Reserve's role in financial intermediation. In particular, the spread between the IOER rate and the ON RRP rate could be set wide enough to discourage very large average ON RRP take-up and reduce the facility's usage in normal times. If the ON RRP rate is significantly below the IOER rate, money market investors are more likely to invest (directly or indirectly) in reserves and less likely to invest in ON RRP—that is, changes in the spread should cause substitution between these two forms of Federal Reserve liabilities. However, setting the ON RRP offering rate too low could also limit the usefulness of an ON RRP facility in helping to control short-term interest rates during normalization.

The spread between the IOER and ON RRP rates also could be adjusted as needed to address the risk that, in times of financial stress, the facility could attract sudden, large inflows that contribute to a reduction in the availability of short-term funding. For example, during such episodes, the ON RRP rate could be lowered to reduce the attractiveness of ON RRPs and diminish their potential for displacing private short-term financing activity.

However, as a tool for limiting potentially disruptive surges in ON RRP usage during periods of financial stress, lowering the ON RRP rate (and thus widening the spread relative to the IOER rate) has several limitations. Importantly, if investors become rate-insensitive during such episodes—demanding safe assets at essentially any rate—reducing the rate may be ineffective in discouraging usage. Moreover, demand for safe assets can increase abruptly in a crisis, so a surge in ON RRP take-up could occur before policymakers can react. Such a surge could have lasting effects, since a loss of funding could quickly put some firms in difficulty, even if ON RRP rates are subsequently adjusted. Of course, rates could be lowered in advance of a potential surge in take-up if stress is seen developing in markets, but a risk in lowering the RRP rate preemptively is that doing so could intensify financial stress if investors interpret a rate reduction as a signal that policymakers expect conditions to worsen.

4.3. Setting a cap on the ON RRP facility's size

An alternative means of addressing concerns about ON RRPs would be to use caps to limit take-up directly. Caps could be set high enough to bind only rarely in normal times, so that the facility can be as effective as possible for setting a floor on short-term interest rates. At the same time, caps could be tight enough to limit the Federal Reserve's role in financial intermediation or reduce the likelihood that a run to an ON RRP facility might contribute to financial instability.

Individual caps vs. an aggregate cap

Caps on daily usage could be set individually for each ON RRP investor or imposed only at the aggregate level of ON RRP take-up. As described in section 2, the FOMC is experimenting with both types of caps during the current ON RRP exercise.

A key advantage of having only individual caps is that they allow each counterparty to know in advance the maximum amount that it can invest at the facility, since the amount would not depend on the behavior of other ON RRP counterparties (as it would with an aggregate cap if it was binding). Unless an additional aggregate cap is also in place, total potential ON RRP usage on any day under a system of individual caps would be the sum of those caps. Individual caps could be set at the same level for each investor or at different levels for different investors or investor types.

An aggregate cap would only limit total ON RRP take-up on a given day. As long as the cap is not binding, individual counterparties could invest as much as they desire in ON RRP, unless take-up is also subject to an individual limit. When an aggregate cap binds, however, individual counterparties would not be guaranteed any particular amount of ON RRP; availability would depend on other counterparties' investment choices.

An aggregate cap on its own could provide a more flexible allocation of usage among counterparties than a system of individual caps. Hence, an aggregate cap may be better suited to allocating ON RRPs to the counterparties that value them most. Similarly, if there is not perfect correlation in individual counterparties' demand, an aggregate cap could allow for a more favorable tradeoff between the objectives of limiting the size of the facility (and the magnitude of potential surges in take-up) and avoiding instances in which caps bind frequently under normal market conditions. For example, an aggregate cap that is expected to bind on a given fraction of days can be set lower than the sum of individual caps that likely would bind for at least one counterparty on the same number of days.[40]

---

[40] For example, consider two counterparties, each of which has ON RRP demand that varies randomly and uniformly from 0 to $10 billion, and assume that their demand is uncorrelated. An aggregate cap for these counterparties set at $10 billion would bind half of the time. If individual caps are each set at $5 billion to maintain the same effective aggregate cap of $10 billion, at least one of the individual caps would bind three-quarters of the

For an aggregate cap, a rule is needed to allocate usage among investors if the cap is reached. In section 4.4, we describe the auction mechanism currently being tested, which operates in the event that the cap is binding. Another possibility would be to ration awards on a pro rata basis based on investors' stated demand, although that approach could lead to overbidding when the cap is expected to bind.

Under an auction-based allocation system, when an aggregate cap is binding, the amount of ON RRPs available to an individual investor is determined by that investor's and others' bids and hence is not completely predictable. As noted above, an advantage of individual caps is that each counterparty would know its potential take-up in advance. In addition to reducing uncertainty during periods of stress, such predictability may help make an ON RRP facility more effective in establishing a floor on short-term interest rates by giving counterparties confidence that a known amount ON RRP is available as a substitute for other investment options.

Static cap vs. dynamic cap

Caps—whether they are set at the individual or aggregate level—could be static or dynamic. Static caps are set in advance and do not vary unless policymakers choose to adjust them. In contrast, dynamic caps would be adjusted at regular intervals (such as daily or weekly), perhaps using a pre-specified rule, which might be based on recent or projected usage. For example, an aggregate dynamic cap could be reset every week at an amount equal to average take-up during the previous week plus a specified amount. Such a cap could be used as a "circuit breaker" that is calibrated to contain potentially disruptive surges in take-up (Dudley 2014).

The dotted blue line in chart 7 illustrates the $300 billion overall limit on take-up that has been in place in the exercise since September 22, 2014 and shows how that limit compares to actual ON RRP take-up in recent months. The solid red line illustrates an example of a dynamic, circuit-breaker cap, which might be employed in addition to (or instead of) a static limit like the $300 billion overall limit in the current exercise. The dynamic cap shown here is equal to average ON RRP usage over the previous five days plus $100 billion, although a variety of formulations would be possible.

More generically, static and dynamic caps have different advantages. A potential advantage of a dynamic cap is that it could be used to control potential one-day surges in ON RRP take-up with more precision than a static limit. (As illustrated in chart 7, potential one-day surges in ON RRP usage would be the gaps between a particular cap on a given day and actual, or "normal," usage on the previous day.) That is, the dynamic, circuit-breaker cap would adjust automatically to accommodate changing demand and market conditions, and it would tend to keep the size of potential jumps in usage within a narrower range. With a static cap, when usage is relatively low, the size of potential surges in take-up could be large. However, if usage is trending high and close to the static cap, the cap may be so tight that it eliminates potential surges but at the expense of the effectiveness of the facility in setting a floor on short-term rates.

---

time. Experience to date with actual take-up patterns corroborates the point that an aggregate cap set at a given level can accommodate ON RRP demand more effectively than a system of individual caps that sum to the same amount.

A static cap offers greater simplicity than a dynamic cap; a static cap at a given level is straightforward and easily described. In addition, a static cap might be better suited than a dynamic cap to limit the Federal Reserve's footprint in short-term funding markets, as the dynamic cap presumably would increase with ON RRP demand. In fact, the circuit-breaker cap illustrated in chart 7 could expand fairly rapidly; for example, if usage were to reach the cap on successive days, the cap could increase by about $70 billion in three days.

Finally, a combination of a static overall limit on usage and a dynamic, circuit-breaker cap might offer the advantages of each form of cap. That is, the static overall limit could address concerns about the Federal Reserve's footprint in short-term funding markets, while the circuit-breaker cap could mitigate financial-stability risks that might be associated with sudden surges in take-up.

4.4. An auction mechanism to allocate usage

On the occasions when an aggregate cap is binding on ON RRP demand, an auction can provide a market-based pricing mechanism to allocate usage to investors that place the highest value on ON RRPs. An auction also might mimic the price dynamics of safe assets during flight-to-quality episodes.

For example, a single-price auction, with a maximum bid rate equal to the ON RRP offering rate, can be used on days when demand exceeds the cap.[41] Indeed, such an auction mechanism has been part of the ON RRP testing exercise since September 22, 2014. Counterparties that wish to invest in ON RRPs must submit both a dollar amount (a bid quantity) and an interest rate. If the sum of dollar bids is less than the aggregate cap, then all counterparties receive the amounts that they have requested at the ON RRP offering rate. If total bids exceed the cap (say, at quarter-end or during a period of stress), bids are ordered from the lowest interest rate bid to the highest, and ON RRPs are allocated to bidders starting with those that bid the lowest rate until the aggregate cap is reached. The auction rate produced by this procedure (that is, the stop-out rate) is the highest rate bid by any counterparty that is awarded a positive amount of ON RRPs.

The "single-price" nature of the auction means that all counterparties that are awarded any ON RRPs receive the same interest rate. Those counterparties that bid a rate below the auction rate receive the dollar amounts that they have requested, and any remaining capacity is divided (on a pro rata basis) among those whose bid rates are equal to the stop-out rate. Ordinarily, the rate produced by this procedure is expected to be the ON RRP offering rate set by the FOMC, but when the cap binds, the auction-determined rate can be lower.

As noted in section 2, the auction mechanism that is part of the current ON RRP testing exercise has been used once to date, on September 30, 2014. Bids totaled $407 billion on that day, so the $300 billon aggregate cap was binding. Although the ON RRP offering rate was 5 basis points that day, the auction resulted in an ON RRP rate of 0 basis points.

---

[41] Uniform-price auctions are currently used for U.S. Treasuries and are also commonly used to conduct initial public offerings.

Chart 8 illustrates more generally how ON RRP rates might vary with demand under a system that includes an aggregate cap and an auction. For quantities of ON RRPs below the cap, the supply curve is the thin blue dashed line in the chart. The thin, solid blue curve, D_{Normal}, represents aggregate demand during normal periods (it is upward-sloping because investors demand more ON RRPs when the *rate* is higher). In normal times, equilibrium take-up is well below the cap and the ON RRP rate is the ON RRP offering rate, that is, the maximum bid rate, R_{Max}.

In a crisis, demand might shift out to the thick, solid red curve, D_{Surge}. Demand at the ON RRP offering rate exceeds the cap, which becomes binding. For demand in excess of the cap, the supply curve is the vertical line at the cap. Total awards when the crisis occurs are limited to the cap, and investors receive the rate set by the auction, $R_{Auction}$, which can fall below the ON RRP offering rate.

5. Tradeoffs in the design of an ON RRP facility

Policymakers may face tradeoffs in designing an ON RRP facility as they seek to balance potentially competing objectives, such as setting an effective floor on money market rates, minimizing the unintended effects of a larger Federal Reserve role in short-term funding markets, and limiting risks to financial stability.

For example, setting the ON RRP rate well below the IOER rate would be one means of limiting the footprint of the ON RRP facility in financial markets, but a wide spread between these two rates may have some drawbacks. For instance, rates on bank loans, such as the "prime rate," may remain tied to the top of the FFR target range and hence linked to the IOER rate, which is an opportunity cost of bank lending, but funding costs in money markets could remain close to the ON RRP rate. A wide spread could contribute to incentives for lending activity to move away from the banking sector. In addition, if the frictions that prevent the IOER rate from exerting a strong upward pull on money market rates vary over time, a wide spread could lead to greater volatility in—and uncertainty about—short-term rates.

Another tradeoff pertains to setting caps on ON RRP usage. Very low limits that often bind could contain the Federal Reserve's footprint in short-term funding markets and virtually eliminate potentially disruptive surges into an ON RRP facility, but such caps also would diminish the effectiveness of ON RRPs in achieving their primary purpose, that is, in helping to establish a floor on short-term interest rates. If the availability of ON RRPs is severely constrained, money market investors will have to look elsewhere for lending opportunities and potentially would be willing to invest at rates that fall well short of the ON RRP rate. By contrast, very high caps set at levels that are never close to binding could allow an ON RRP facility to set a firmer floor on interest rates. But such high caps may not do enough to address concerns that a large ON RRP facility could expand the Federal Reserve's role in short-term intermediation and potentially pose a threat to financial stability.

These tradeoffs are also likely to evolve. For example, the full implementation of new capital and liquidity rules in coming years may drive up financial institutions' costs of short-term funding and diminish their demand for receiving this type of financing. This could reduce the availability of money market instruments and boost demand for ON RRPs. If so, all else equal, a larger ON RRP facility may be needed to prevent a widening of spreads between the IOER rate and other short-term interest rates. Moreover, in such a scenario, the falloff in private borrowers' demand for short-term funding may diminish concerns about crowding out such funding.

In addition, policy normalization itself may affect the tradeoffs. With the FOMC's target range for the FFR currently set at zero to ¼ percent, structural features of the money markets that impede nominal interest rates from falling below zero are probably helping to keep short-term interest rates in the target range. Once the bottom end of the target range is raised above zero, monetary policy tools that are intended to set a floor for short-term interest rates, such as an ON RRP facility, may need to be relied upon more heavily.

Some of the tradeoffs in policy goals might be addressed by adopting design features that balance objectives effectively. For instance, as noted in section 4, an aggregate cap of the type currently being tested may be more effective than individual counterparty caps in addressing some of the concerns about an ON RRP facility that are described in this paper. That is, an aggregate cap can be set at a level that is rarely binding but which allows a smaller footprint and smaller potential surges than a system of individual caps that binds with the same frequency.[42] Moreover, an appropriate balancing of objectives could be fostered by the timing of implementation of some of the features of the facility. For example, the Committee may wish to temporarily employ a sizeable ON RRP cap at the commencement of policy normalization to ensure a successful process, while announcing a strategy to lower the cap over time and eventually phase out the facility. Indeed, when the Committee would want to start normalization, economic and financial conditions will be unlikely to be associated with heightened risk of a disruptive flight-to-quality event.

Tests of ON RRPs conducted to date have been designed, in part, to provide a better understanding of the trade-offs involved in pursuing various policy goals. Information garnered from these tests will be helpful in the design of an ON RRP facility that can achieve the FOMC's desired level of interest rate control during the normalization process while addressing the concerns related to financial stability and the Federal Reserve's footprint in short-term funding markets.

6. Conclusions

An ON RRP facility offers a promising technical advance in the implementation of monetary policy. By making ON RRPs available to a broad set of investors, including nonbank institutions that are significant lenders in money markets, such a facility can complement the use of IOER and help control short-term interest rates. Indeed, the FOMC has stated that it intends to use an ON RRP facility for this purpose during the policy normalization process.

At the same time, an ON RRP facility may have important secondary effects with both positive and negative implications. The FOMC has considered a range of issues associated with an ON

---

[42] Even so, limits on individual counterparty usage may be useful for other reasons, such as for preserving access to ON RRPs for a relatively broad range of counterparties.

RRP facility and has directed the Desk to test several design features of ON RRP operations, including some which might be used to address undesirable secondary effects. Results of the testing exercise in place since September 2013 have been quite encouraging and indicate that even capped offerings of ON RRPs can be effective in setting a floor for short-term interest rates. FOMC policymakers have generally agreed upon the importance of a successful commencement of the policy normalization process, and they have indicated that they will be prepared take the steps necessary to keep the federal funds rate within the target range established by the Committee (FOMC 2015).

Appendix

This appendix supplements sections 3.2.3 and 3.2.4 of the paper. Section A.1 adds to the analysis of section 3.2.3, which examines flight-to-quality dynamics in September 2008, by reviewing evidence from two more recent and more modest flight-to-quality episodes. Section A.2 furthers the discussion in section 3.2.4 by reviewing MMF portfolio data to provide additional detail on the nature of the institutions and firms that might lose short-term funding quickly amidst a large-scale flight-to-quality event.

A.1. The dynamics of additional flight-to-quality events

The two additional flight-to-quality episodes are the debt-ceiling standoffs of July-August 2011 and October 2013. As was the case for the September 2008 example, we focus here on flows that occurred during a one-week window during each episode.

During the debt-ceiling episodes of 2011 and 2013, large safe-haven flows went primarily to banks, as investors shunned some government securities. As illustrated in charts A1 and A2, liquid deposits surged $270 billion in the week ending August 1, 2011, and they increased $120 billion in the week ending October 16, 2013.[43]

Run dynamics occurred on a more modest scale during the 2011 and 2013 episodes than in 2008, and the direction of some flows differed, too. The risk of delays in Treasury payments led to flight-to-quality flows *from* government MMFs. In the week ending on August 1, 2011, both prime *and* government MMFs experienced outflows—each about $60 billion—and CP outstanding dropped $50 billion. In the five business days ending on October 16, 2013, net redemptions from prime and government MMFs totaled $15 billion and $40 billion, respectively, and CP outstanding declined $20 billion.

As noted in the text, changes in the perception of the relative risk of various investments may lead to sharp differences in flow patterns during flights to quality. The debt-ceiling episodes illustrate this point. Government MMFs, which attracted very large inflows in 2008, saw outflows in 2011 and 2013, when government securities were themselves a source of concern.

A.2. Using MMF portfolio holdings data to identify the institutions and firms that might lose short-term funding quickly amidst a large-scale flight-to-quality event

As noted in section 3.2.4, the effects of changes in flight-to-quality flows on financial stability and economic activity would depend in large part on the nature of the institutions and firms that might lose short-term funding as investors shift to ON RRPs. The short-term assets held by MMFs provide one perspective on the composition of borrowers that might be at risk. On average in 2014, 90 percent of the $540 billion in financing that matured within a week from ON

---

[43] For the 2011 episode, we focus on the period in late July and early August, when concerns about the debt-ceiling standoff appear to have motivated widespread flight-to-quality flows. Earlier that summer, prime MMFs had experienced heavy outflows amid concerns about their large European exposures.

RRP-counterparty MMFs went to 43 recipients.[44] Forty-one of these recipients were banks and their subsidiaries, including broker-dealers, and 34 were foreign banks. The ultimate recipients of this financing are less certain, but they would have included clients, such as hedge funds and nonfinancial firms, that normally obtain funding from the banks and broker-dealers. For example, $270 billion of the one-week funding was repo, which might have been used to finance collateral for a variety of borrowers.

---

[44] These figures are based on average funding for each recipient reported at month-ends from January to December 2014. The financing considered here excludes Federal Reserve RRPs and Treasury securities.

References

Carlson, Mark, Burcu Duygan-Bump, Fabio Natalucci, William R. Nelson, Marcelo Ochoa, Jeremy Stein, and Skander Van den Heuvel, 2014, "The Demand for Short-Term, Safe Assets and Financial Stability: Some Evidence and Implications for Central Bank Policies," Federal Reserve Board Finance and Economics Discussion Series Working Paper no. 2014-102 (November 25). www.federalreserve.gov/econresdata/feds/2014/files/2014102pap.pdf.

Cipriani, Marco, Antoine Martin, Patrick McCabe, and Bruno M. Parigi, 2014, "Gates, Fees, and Preemptive Runs," Federal Reserve Bank of New York Staff Report No. 670 (April). www.newyorkfed.org/research/staff_reports/sr670.pdf.

Diamond, Douglas W. and Philip H. Dybvig, 1983, "Bank Runs, Deposit Insurance, and Liquidity," *Journal of Political Economy* 91:3 (June), 401-419.

Dudley, William, 2014, "The Economic Outlook and Implications for Monetary Policy," Remarks before the New York Association for Business Economics, New York City (May 20). www.newyorkfed.org/newsevents/speeches/2014/dud140520.html.

Ennis, Huberto M. and Todd Keister, 2006, "Bank Runs and Investment Decisions Revisited," *Journal of Monetary Economics* 53:2 (March), 217-232.

____, 2008, "Understanding Monetary Policy Implementation," *Federal Reserve Bank of Richmond Economic Quarterly* 94:3 (Summer), 235-263.

Federal Open Market Committee (FOMC), 2013a, "Minutes of the Federal Open Market Committee" (July 30-31). www.federalreserve.gov/monetarypolicy/files/fomcminutes20130731.pdf.

____, 2013b, "Minutes of the Federal Open Market Committee" (September 17-18). www.federalreserve.gov/monetarypolicy/files/fomcminutes20130918.pdf.

____, 2014a, "Minutes of the Federal Open Market Committee" (June 17-18). www.federalreserve.gov/monetarypolicy/files/fomcminutes20140618.pdf.

____, 2014b, "Minutes of the Federal Open Market Committee" (July 29-30). www.federalreserve.gov/monetarypolicy/files/fomcminutes20140730.pdf.

____, 2014c, "Policy Normalization Principles and Plans" (September 17). www.federalreserve.gov/newsevents/press/monetary/20140917c.htm.

____, 2014d, "Minutes of the Federal Open Market Committee," (September 16-17). www.federalreserve.gov/monetarypolicy/files/fomcminutes20140917.pdf.

____, 2015, "Minutes of the Federal Open Market Committee," (January 27-28). www.federalreserve.gov/monetarypolicy/files/fomcminutes20150128.pdf.

Federal Reserve Bank of New York, 2013, "Statement Regarding Overnight Fixed-Rate Reverse Repurchase Agreement Operational Exercise" (September 20). www.newyorkfed.org/markets/opolicy/operating_policy_130920.html.

____, 2014a, "Statement to Revise the Terms of the Overnight Reverse Repurchase Agreement Operational Exercise" (September 17). www.newyorkfed.org/markets/opolicy/operating_policy_140917.html.

____, 2014b, "Statement Regarding Reverse Repurchase Agreements" (October 29). www.newyorkfed.org/markets/opolicy/operating_policy_141029.html.

____, 2014c, "Statement Regarding Reverse Repurchase Transaction Counterparty Applications" (November 12). www.newyorkfed.org/markets/opolicy/operating_policy_141112.html.

____, 2015, "Statement Regarding Term Reverse Repurchase Agreements" (January 28). www.newyorkfed.org/markets/opolicy/operating_policy_150128.html.

Gagnon, Joseph E. and Brian Sack, 2014, "Monetary Policy with Abundant Liquidity: A New Operating Framework for the Federal Reserve," Peterson Institute for International Economics Policy Brief (January). www.iie.com/publications/pb/pb14-4.pdf.

Gatev, Evan, Til Schuermann, and Philip E. Strahan, 2009, "Managing Bank Liquidity Risk: How Deposit-Loan Synergies Vary with Market Conditions," *The Review of Financial Studies* 22:3 (March), 995-1020.

Gorton, Gary and Andrew Metrick, 2012, "Securitized banking and the run on repo," *Journal of Financial Economics* 104:3 (June), 425-451.

Greenwood, Robin, Samuel G. Hanson, and Jeremy C. Stein, 2013, "A Comparative-Advantage Approach to Government Debt Maturity," mimeo (September).

Kahn, George A., 2010, "Monetary Policy under a Corridor Operating Framework," *Federal Reserve Bank of Kansas City Economic Review* (Fourth Quarter), 5-34.

Keister, Todd, Antoine Martin, and James McAndrews, 2008, "Divorcing Money from Monetary Policy," *Federal Reserve Bank of New York Economic Policy Review* 14:2 (September), 41-56.

Krishnamurthy, Arvind and Annette Vissing-Jorgensen, 2013, "Short-term Debt and Financial Crises: What We Can Learn from U.S. Treasury Supply," mimeo (May).

Morris and Shin, 2010, "Illiquidity Component of Credit Risk," Princeton University, mimeo (February).

Stein, Jeremy C., 2012, "Monetary Policy as Financial Stability Regulation," *Quarterly Journal of Economics* 127:1 (February), 57–95.

U.S. Securities and Exchange Commission, 2013, "Money Market Fund Reform; Amendments to Form PF: Proposed Rule." Release no. 33-9408 (June 5). www.sec.gov/rules/proposed/2013/33-9408.pdf.

Wrightson ICAP, 2014, "The Fed's Overnight RRP Program," *The Money Market Observer* (February 24), 4-7.

Chart 1. Selected money market rates

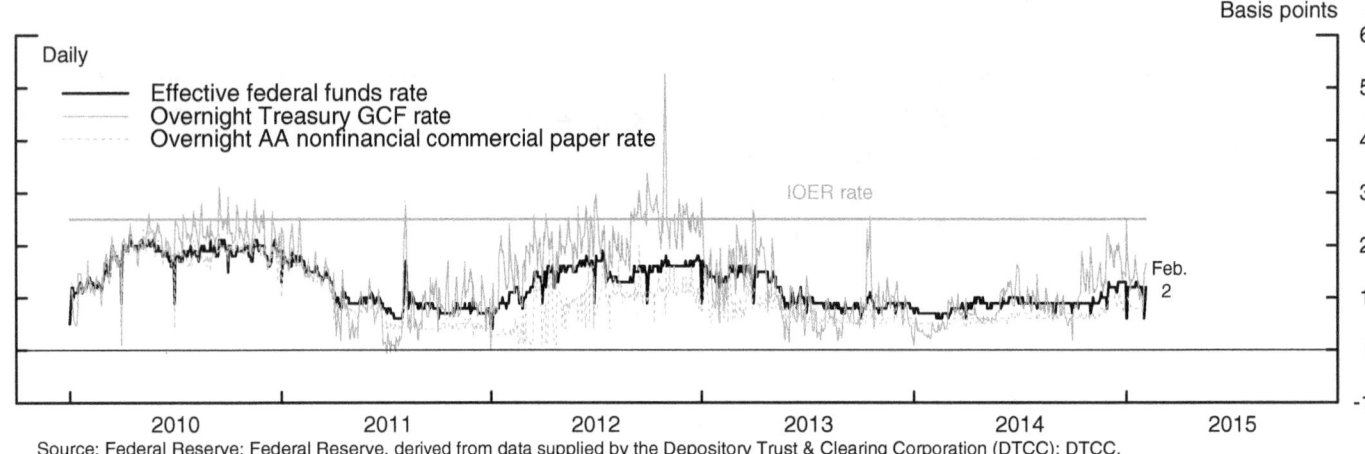

Source: Federal Reserve; Federal Reserve, derived from data supplied by the Depository Trust & Clearing Corporation (DTCC); DTCC.

Chart 2. Selected money market rates, including the ON RRP offering rate

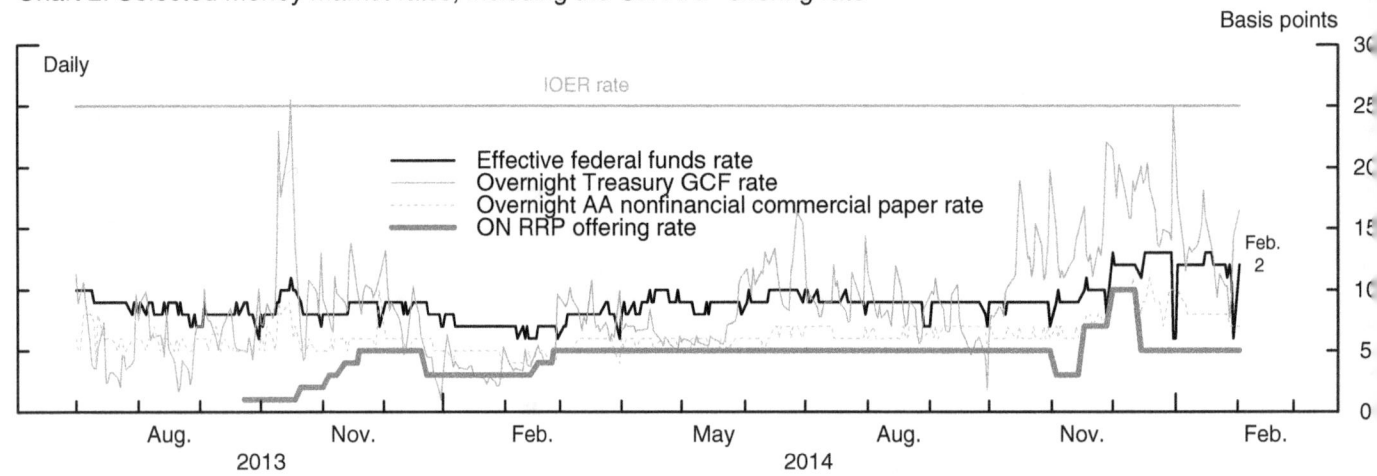

Source: Federal Reserve; Federal Reserve, derived from data supplied by the Depository Trust & Clearing Corporation (DTCC); DTCC.

Chart 3. ON RRP take-up and caps

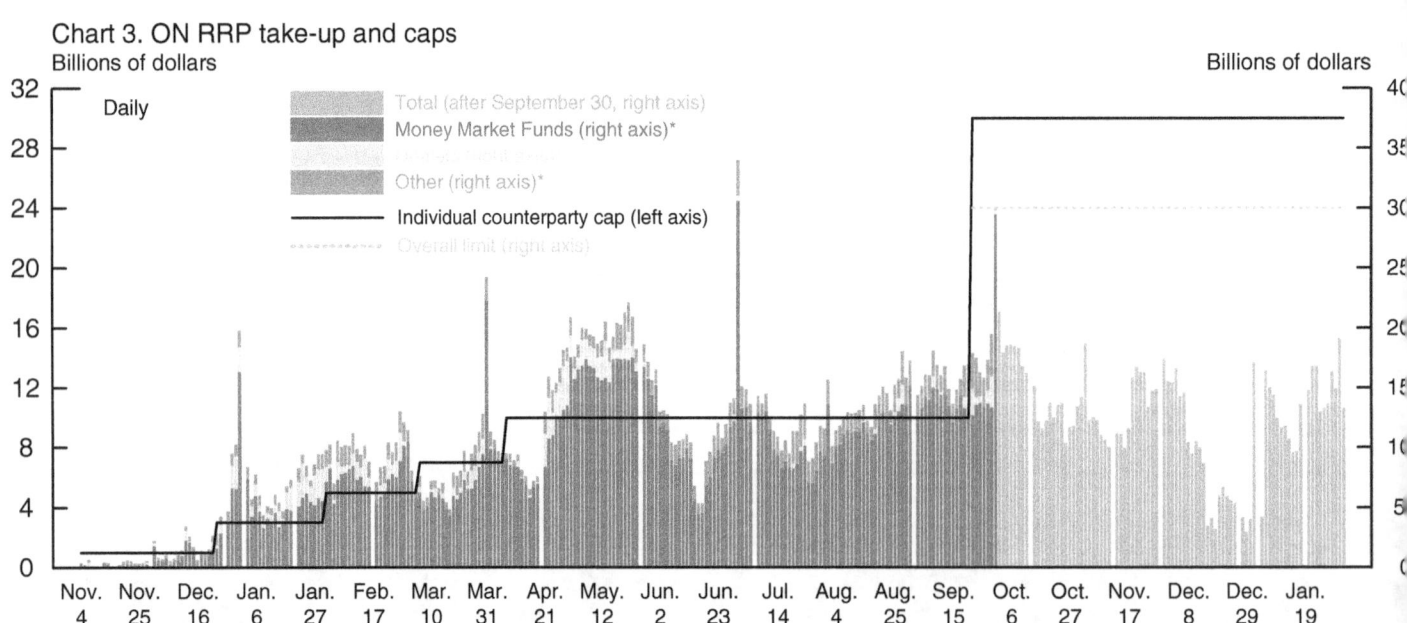

Source: Federal Reserve Bank of New York.
* Counterparty-type data are publicly available through September 30, 2014.

Chart 4. ON RRP take-up versus spread to Treasury GCF rate

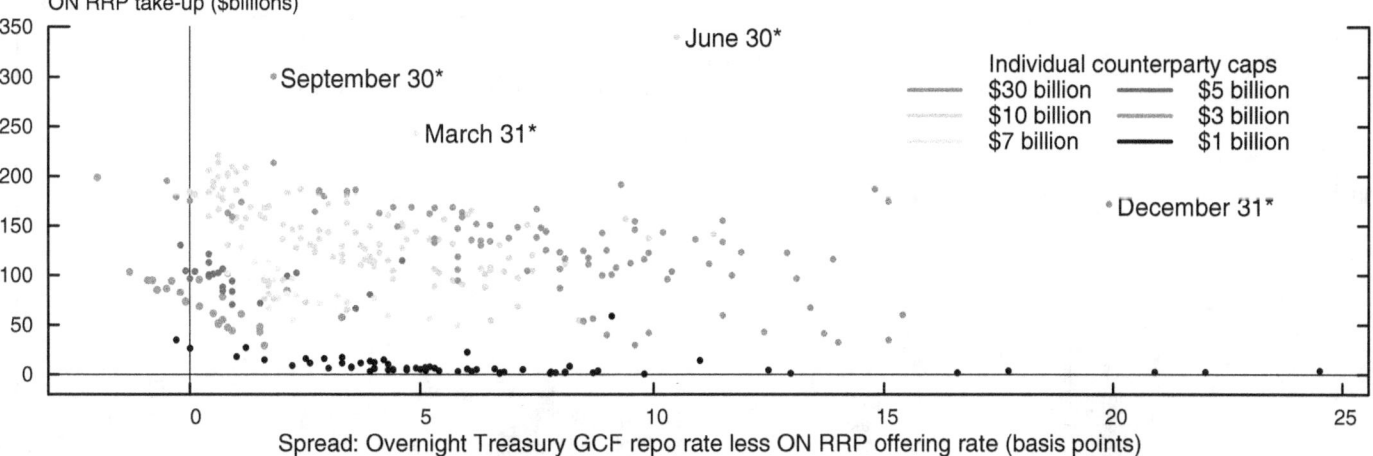

ON RRP take-up ($billions)

Individual counterparty caps
- $30 billion
- $10 billion
- $7 billion
- $5 billion
- $3 billion
- $1 billion

June 30*

September 30*

March 31*

December 31*

Spread: Overnight Treasury GCF repo rate less ON RRP offering rate (basis points)

Source: Federal Reserve Bank of New York, DTCC.
*2014.

Chart 5. Money market fund holdings of repo collateralized with U.S. government securities

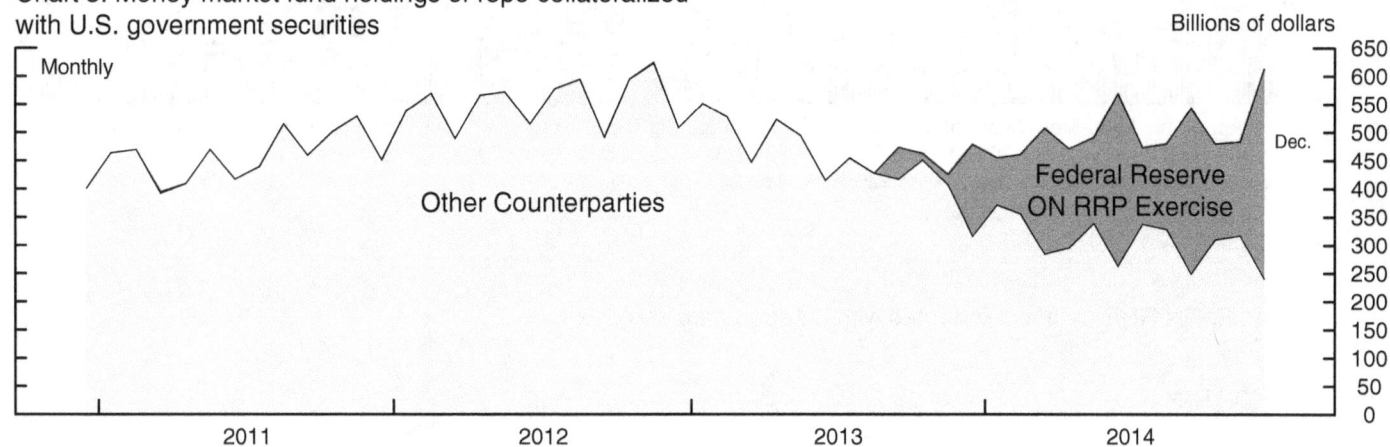

Billions of dollars

Monthly

Other Counterparties

Federal Reserve ON RRP Exercise

Dec.

2011   2012   2013   2014

Source: Securities and Exchange Commission form N-MFP filings.

Chart 7. Illustration of ON RRP take-up and static and dynamic caps

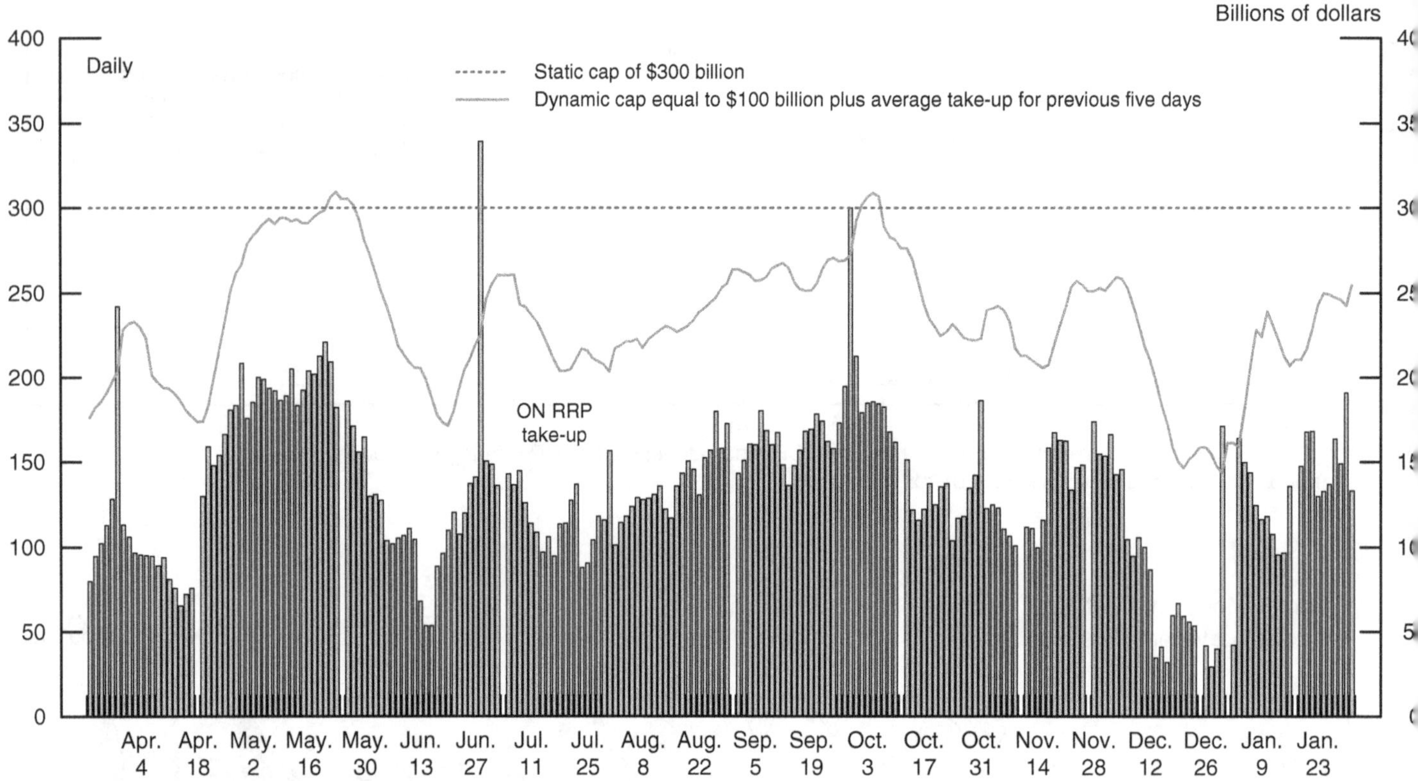

Billions of dollars

Daily

- - - - - Static cap of $300 billion
——— Dynamic cap equal to $100 billion plus average take-up for previous five days

ON RRP
take-up

Apr.	Apr.	May.	May.	May.	Jun.	Jun.	Jul.	Jul.	Aug.	Aug.	Sep.	Sep.	Oct.	Oct.	Oct.	Nov.	Nov.	Dec.	Dec.	Jan.	Jan.
4	18	2	16	30	13	27	11	25	8	22	5	19	3	17	31	14	28	12	26	9	23

Source: Federal Reserve Bank of New York and authors' calculations.

Chart 8. ON RRP demand and rates with an aggregate cap

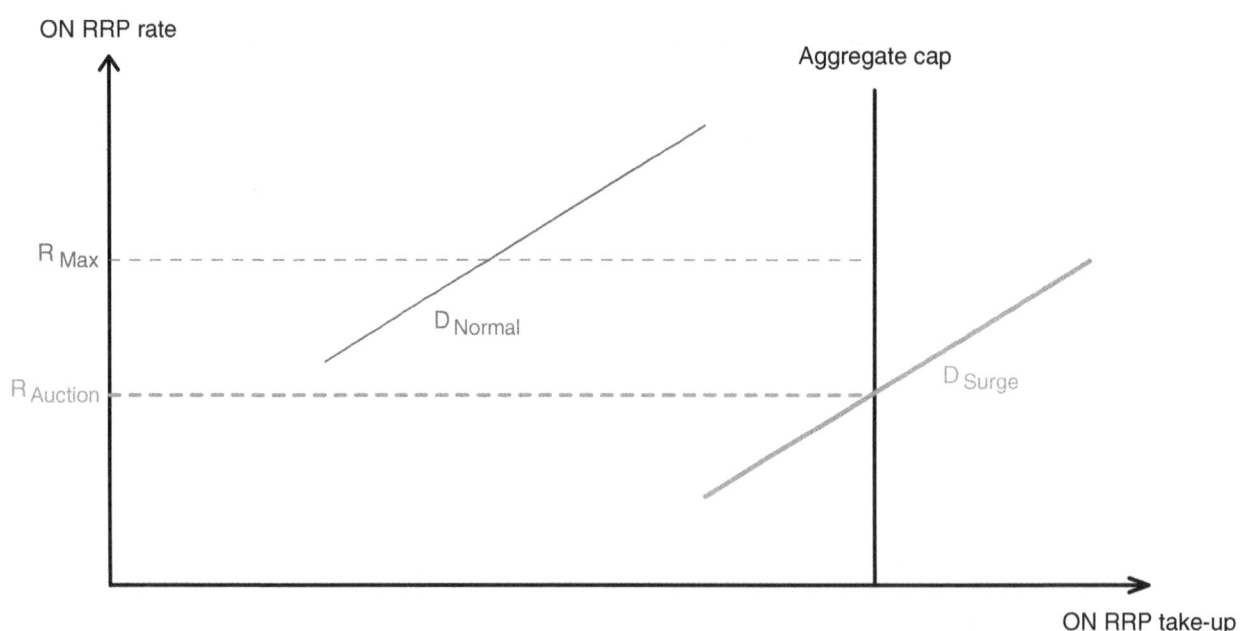